DATE DUE

SEP 1 2 2002	
NOV 1 2 2002 DEC 0 4 2002	
OCT 1 3 2005 FEB 1 7 2006	Sale
JUL 1 1 2007	
MAR 2 4 2010	
APR 3 0 2010	
FEB 1 1 2011	
MAY 0 7 2013	

★ *GREAT SPORTS TEAMS* ★

THE DALLAS

COWBOYS

FOOTBALL TEAM

William W. Lace

Enslow Publishers, Inc.

40 Industrial Road	PO Box 38
Box 398	Aldershot
Berkeley Heights, NJ 07922	Hants GU12 6BP
USA	UK

http://www.enslow.com

Library of Congress Cataloging-in-Publication Data

Lace, William W.
     The Dallas Cowboys football team / William W. Lace.
         p. cm. — (Great sports teams)
     Includes bibliographical references.
     Summary: Covers the history of the professional football franchise known
as "America's team," discussing some key players, coaches, and important
games, as well as efforts by Jimmy Johnson and Jerry Jones to rebuild the
team.
     ISBN 0-89490-791-3
     1. Dallas Cowboys (Football team)—History—Juvenile literature. [1. Dallas
Cowboys (Football team) 2. Football—History.]
     I. Title. II. Series.
GV956.D3L33 1997
796.332'64'097642812—dc20   96-26411
                                                                CIP
                                                                AC

Printed in the United States of America

10 9 8 7 6 5 4 3

To Our Readers:
All Internet addresses in this book were active and appropriate when we
went to press. Any comments or suggestions can be sent by e-mail to
Comments@enslow.com or to the address on the back cover.

Illustration Credits: AP/Wide World Photos, pp. 4, 7, 8, 10, 13, 14, 16, 19, 20, 22,
25, 26, 28, 31, 32, 34, 37, 38.

Cover Illustration: AP/Wide World Photos.

CONTENTS

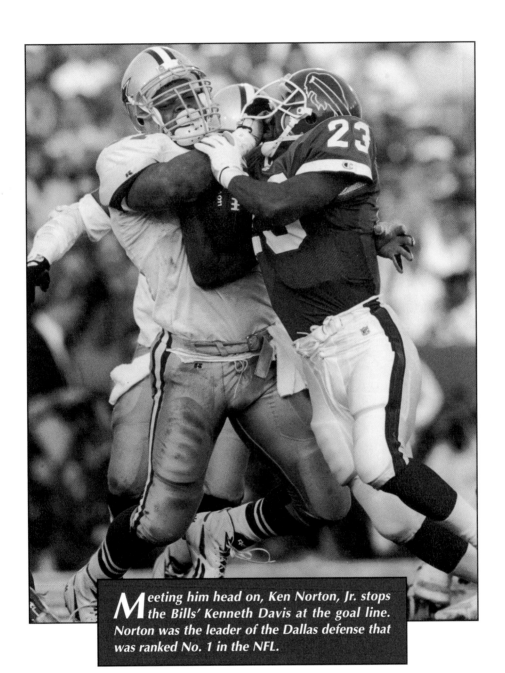

*M*eeting him head on, Ken Norton, Jr. stops the Bills' Kenneth Davis at the goal line. Norton was the leader of the Dallas defense that was ranked No. 1 in the NFL.

THE BOYS ARE BACK

Jimmy Johnson, head coach of the Dallas Cowboys, was getting nervous. Only four minutes remained in the National Football Conference championship game on January 17, 1993. Earlier in the fourth quarter, the Cowboys had gone for a touchdown instead of a field goal on fourth down from the San Francisco 49ers' 7-yard line, and missed. Now, the 49ers had scored to cut the Cowboys' lead to four points.

The Cowboys had the ball on their own 21-yard line. Would they play it safe and try to run out the clock? That wasn't Johnson's style. "Do what you have to do to win this thing," he told offensive coordinator Norv Turner.[1]

On first down, Turner called for wide receiver Alvin Harper to run a pass pattern known as "skinny post 8." Harper ran straight down the field, then cut sharply across the middle. He took a perfectly thrown pass from quarterback Troy Aikman and dashed all the way to the 49er 9-yard line. Three plays later, Aikman threw a touchdown pass to Kelvin Martin.

An Excited Coach

On the sideline, Johnson bounced up and down like an excited fourth-grader. After the game, he stood on a locker room chair and yelled, "How 'bout them Cowboys?"[2] His players roared their approval. They were going to the Super Bowl!

Later, reporters asked Johnson about Harper's big play. "That's been kind of our style all year," Johnson said. "From the opening whistle, we were going to play aggressive football in all phases of the game."[3]

The Cowboys had come a long way to earn their spot in Super Bowl XXVII. It had been fourteen long years since Dallas, one of the most successful teams in National Football League history, had been to the championship. In 1989, Johnson's first year as coach, the Cowboys won only one game. Johnson and owner Jerry Jones built the team with good draft choices and smart trades, making forty-six trades in four seasons. In 1991, Dallas made the playoffs for the first time since 1985. In 1992, they were going all the way.

Making History

"This is history in the making," Jones said after the game.[4] Only one thing stood in the Cowboys' way—the Buffalo Bills. The Bills had beaten the Miami Dolphins to win the American Football Conference championship and now would play Dallas in the Super Bowl in the Rose Bowl in Pasadena, California.

The Dallas Cowboys Football Team

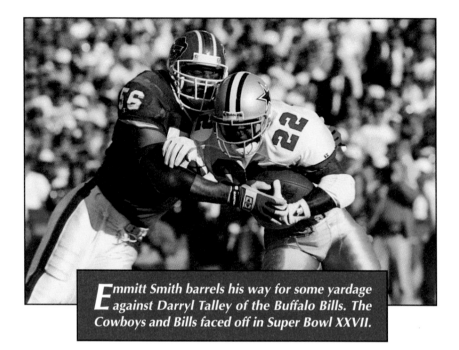

Emmitt Smith barrels his way for some yardage against Darryl Talley of the Buffalo Bills. The Cowboys and Bills faced off in Super Bowl XXVII.

Dallas was made a seven-point favorite. Many experts, however, thought that Buffalo, going to its third straight Super Bowl, would win because of its experience. The Cowboys, they said, would be nervous and would make mistakes. Jones wasn't worried. "We'll be at a disadvantage in experience," he said. "Haven't we heard that before?"[5]

It turned out to be the Bills, however, who made the mistakes. After Buffalo took a 7–0 lead, the Cowboys turned three pass interceptions and two fumble recoveries into a 28–10 halftime advantage. From there, they cruised to a 52–17 rout.

The Defense Shines

It was a great day for the Dallas defense. Even though they had finished the season ranked first in the NFL,

*J*immy Johnson receives an unexpected shower on the sidelines near the end of Super Bowl XXVII. The Cowboys blew out the Bills, 52–17.

they were snubbed in the Pro Bowl voting. Not a single defensive player was named to the Pro Bowl. "We're somebody now," said linebacker Ken Norton, Jr.[6]

The offense had a big day, too. Aikman, voted the game's Most Valuable Player, passed for 273 yards, and Emmitt Smith ran for 108 yards. Michael Irvin caught 6 passes for 114 yards and 2 touchdowns.

"Get used to the Dallas Cowboys, folks," one reporter wrote, "because they're going to be with us for a long time."[7]

Sure enough, the Cowboys came right back the next year and made it two Super Bowls in a row, beating the Bills again, 30–13. Clearly, the Cowboys were well on their way to becoming the team of the 1990s.

*B*lasting through the hole, the Cowboys' L.G. Dupre scores a touchdown. The Cowboys played their first season in 1960. Things got off to a rough start as the team finished 0-11-1.

2

AMERICA'S TEAM

The Dallas Cowboys were born because not one, but two Dallas millionaires wanted to be pro football owners. The first was Lamar Hunt. He had tried to buy an NFL team but was not successful, so, instead, he announced in 1959 that he would form his own league—the American Football League (AFL). Hunt's own team would be the Dallas Texans.

The second man was Clint Murchison. Murchison also had tried to buy several NFL teams but failed. The NFL, however, did not want the AFL to succeed. It wanted to put an NFL team in Dallas to compete with Hunt's Texans. On January 20, 1960, the NFL voted to award a team to Murchison. At first, he named his team the Rangers. Later, because there was a minor-league baseball team in Texas also named the Rangers, he renamed his team the Dallas Cowboys.

The Cowboys and the Texans competed for the fans' support for three seasons. Neither team did well in attendance. Finally, in 1963, Hunt moved his team to Kansas City, where it became the Chiefs.

Building a Team

Murchison had not waited for the NFL's formal decision before starting to build his team. To run the operation, he hired Texas E. "Tex" Schramm, who had been with the Los Angeles Rams and was then working for a television network. Schramm's first office was a borrowed desk in a corner of the Texas Auto Club. "People would crowd in there to map routes for trips, and I'd be over in a corner discussing player contracts on the phone. Sometimes they'd listen in. The noise was unbelievable."[1]

Getting players was a problem, since the Cowboys entered the NFL too late to participate in the 1960 college draft. Instead, each team placed some of its less talented or older players on a list from which the Cowboys could choose. Most didn't last long, but two—linebacker Jerry Tubbs and receiver Frank Clarke—would be All-Pro players.

Signing a Quarterback

One of the first Cowboys was quarterback Don Meredith from Southern Methodist University in Dallas. To make sure that they would get Meredith— and that the Texans wouldn't—Murchison signed him to a private contract even before he officially had a team. He did the same thing with running back Don Perkins. Since Murchison could not participate in the 1960 player draft, he had arranged for other NFL teams to draft these players for him.

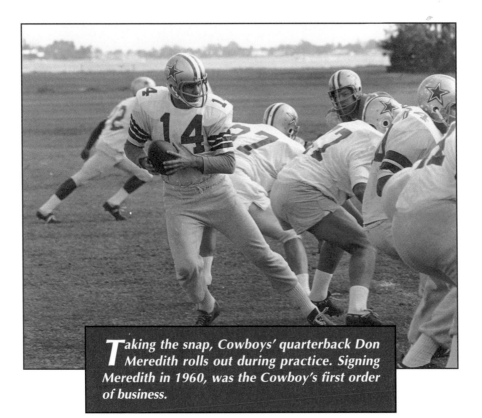

*T*aking the snap, Cowboys' quarterback Don Meredith rolls out during practice. Signing Meredith in 1960, was the Cowboy's first order of business.

When Schramm began looking for a head coach, people told him to consider Tom Landry, a Texas native and a New York Giants assistant. "People were calling him a young genius for what he had done with the Giants' defense," Schramm said. "He was the only person I actually ever talked to about the job."[2] He hired Landry, who thus, at thirty-five, became the youngest head coach in the NFL at that time.

A Slow Start

Schramm, Landry, and chief scout Gil Brandt did what they could to put a team together for the 1960 season, but it wasn't much of a team. It lost every

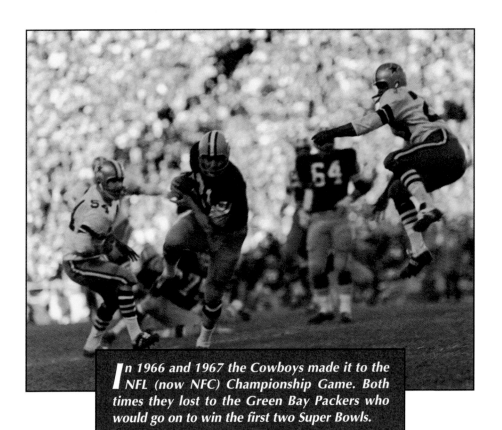

In 1966 and 1967 the Cowboys made it to the NFL (now NFC) Championship Game. Both times they lost to the Green Bay Packers who would go on to win the first two Super Bowls.

game except for a 31–31 tie with the Giants. Home attendance was terrible. Only about ten thousand fans showed up for the last home game against San Francisco.

For years, the Cowboys were near the bottom of the league. They won only 18 of 68 games during their first five seasons. Slowly, however, draft choices began to pay off—defensive tackle Bob Lilly in 1961, linebacker Lee Roy Jordan in 1963, defensive back Mel Renfro, receiver Bob Hayes, and quarterback Roger Staubach in 1964. By 1966, Dallas was a power in the league.

The Cowboys lost the NFL championship to Green Bay in both 1966 and 1967 and lost Super Bowl V to Baltimore in 1972. Their fans cried that they "couldn't win the big one." The Cowboys took care of that in 1973, defeating Miami in Super Bowl VI.

By 1978, Dallas had added a second Super Bowl victory. People not just in Texas, but all over the country became Cowboy fans. NFL Films noticed and, in its Cowboy highlights film, gave the club the nickname by which it would become famous—America's Team.

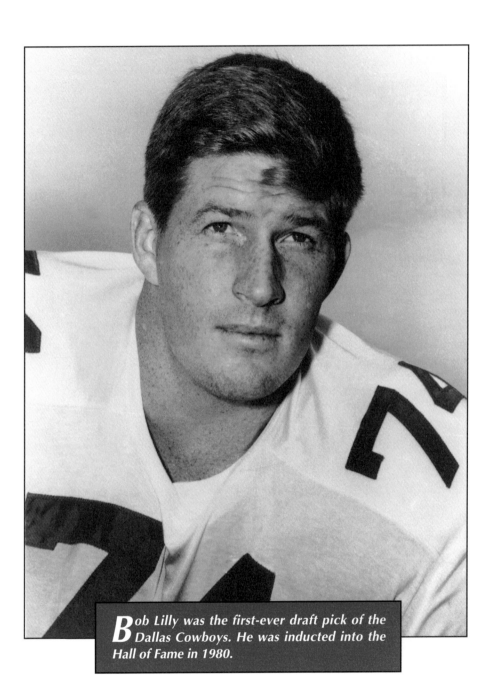

*B*ob Lilly was the first-ever draft pick of the Dallas Cowboys. He was inducted into the Hall of Fame in 1980.

THE GREAT ONES

Since their birth in 1960, the Dallas Cowboys have perhaps had more outstanding players than any other NFL team. Bob Lilly, Tony Dorsett, Roger Staubach, and Randy White are in the Pro Football Hall of Fame. Emmitt Smith and Troy Aikman appear to be headed there.

Bob Lilly

Lilly, Dallas's first-ever draft choice, first played defensive end for the Cowboys but was soon moved to defensive tackle. "I felt more at home," he said. "Being head-up on a man and being able to play him is my kind of football."[1]

Lilly soon developed into one of the NFL's fiercest pass rushers. In Super Bowl VI, he personally made life miserable for Miami quarterback Bob Griese. Toward the end of the first quarter, Lilly shot through a gap in the offensive line and began chasing Griese.

Whichever way the quarterback turned, there was Lilly. At last, Griese was dropped, for a 29-yard loss.

When he made the Hall of Fame in 1980, his coach, Tom Landry, said, "A player like Bob Lilly comes along just about once in a lifetime."[2]

Roger Staubach

Because Staubach had to serve four years in the Navy after graduation from the Naval Academy, NFL teams were reluctant to draft him even though he was a winner of the Heisman Trophy. The Cowboys decided to take a chance, picking him in the tenth round in 1964 .

Staubach was worth the wait. He led the Cowboys to two Super Bowl victories, earning Most Valuable Player (MVP) honors in Super Bowl VI.

Twenty-three times Staubach brought the Cowboys from behind to win. None was more dramatic than on December 28, 1974, when Dallas won a playoff game, 17–14, over Minnesota.

Dallas trailed, 14–10, and had the ball at midfield with only thirty seconds left in the game. Staubach faked a throw, freezing Minnesota safety Paul Krause, then lofted a pass far downfield. Drew Pearson outfought Nate Wright for the ball and crossed the goal line with twenty-six seconds left. The play has gone down in history as the Hail Mary pass.

Tony Dorsett

Dorsett, from the University of Pittsburgh, was the Cowboys' number one draft choice in 1977. "I saw his ability from the first day," said Dan Reeves, then a

The Dallas Cowboys Football Team

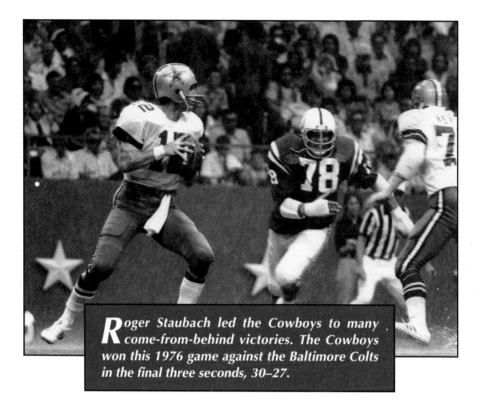

*R*oger Staubach led the Cowboys to many come-from-behind victories. The Cowboys won this 1976 game against the Baltimore Colts in the final three seconds, 30–27.

Dallas assistant coach. "He was just a blur against the linebackers."[3]

In his eleven seasons with Dallas, Dorsett gained more than a thousand yards eight times. His career total of 12,739 yards is the third-best in NFL history.

Dorsett's most famous play came on January 3, 1983. The Cowboys were backed up on their own 1-yard-line. Dorsett took a handoff from Danny White and popped through the line into the open field. He got a block from Pearson, managed to avoid being knocked out of bounds by a Viking defender, and wound up with a 99-yard touchdown. Since, statistically, the ball

Tony Dorsett breaks through the tackles of Carl Ekern (left) and Gary Jeter (77) to gain a first down. When Dorsett retired he was second on the NFL's all-time rushing list.

cannot be closer to the goal than the 1-yard-line, Dorsett's record for the longest touchdown run in NFL history can be tied but never broken.

Randy White

White was a star lineman at the University of Maryland, but the Cowboys tried to make him a linebacker in 1975. After two seasons, he was moved to defensive tackle, where he became a star, earning All-Pro honors eight times. He was co-MVP in Super Bowl XII.

At 263 pounds, White was small as defensive linemen go. He made up for it with great speed. "It didn't seem fair to opponents," one writer said, "that a man who was widely known as the strongest Cowboy could also be one of the fastest."[4]

Emmitt Smith

Smith has turned into pro football's top running back since he joined the Cowboys from Florida in 1990, leading the NFL in rushing 4 times in his first six seasons.

One teammate said that when Smith gets near the goal line, "he's like a pit bull on a sirloin steak."[5] He loves to score touchdowns, and he scored an NFL record 25 in 1995. In only six years, he became the tenth leading rusher in pro football history, with 8,956 yards.

Troy Aikman

Aikman, a UCLA product, was the top player taken in the 1989 draft and is the only rookie quarterback ever to start for the Cowboys.

While he can throw the long pass, Aikman is best known for his amazing accuracy. In 1993, he led the NFL by completing 69.1 percent of his passes while throwing only 6 interceptions. He topped off the year by tossing 4 touchdown passes in the Super Bowl victory over Buffalo, and he was named Most Valuable Player.

*T*ex Schramm poses for photographers at the 1991 Hall of Fame induction ceremony. Tex Schramm is the man that built the Cowboys' organization.

THE MEN AT THE TOP

Two men—Tex Schramm and Tom Landry—built the Dallas Cowboys into champions by the 1970s. Two more—Jerry Jones and Jimmy Johnson—guided the team's return to greatness in the 1990s.

Tex Schramm

Schramm's dream was to run a brand-new team. When he got the opportunity to do so in his home state of Texas, he jumped at the chance. "I wanted to start something from scratch and build it into a success," he said.[1]

Many things Schramm did have since been copied by most other teams. The Cowboys were the first to put scouting reports on a computer. They produced their own television show and newspaper. The famous Dallas Cowboys Cheerleaders were Schramm's idea. He was the mastermind behind the building of

Texas Stadium and of the use of instant replay in officiating.

"When you talk about the success of the Cowboys," said Landry, "you have to remember that Tex built the organization."[2]

Tom Landry

On the field, however, it was Landry who built the Cowboys. Football decisions were his alone, and he made some great ones. He developed the 4–3 defense (four linemen, three linebackers) while he was with the New York Giants. For the Cowboys, he devised the multiple offense, which featured formations constantly shifting to confuse defenses.

As an assistant coach for the New York Giants, he spent countless hours analyzing opponents and going over game films with his players. "I learned more in a few hours with Tom than I'd learned playing football all my life," said linebacker Sam Huff.[3]

Landry's hours of study paid off in 1978 when the Cowboys defeated Minnesota to advance to Super Bowl XII. Watching films, he had noticed that Vikings cornerback Bobby Bryant came upfield quickly on screen passes. During the game, Landry called a play on which Staubach faked a screen pass to Drew Pearson. When Bryant started toward Pearson, Cowboys wide receiver Golden Richards, who had run downfield to throw a block, sped past Bryant. Staubach hit him with a perfect 32-yard touchdown pass.

Landry often appeared cold and unemotional on the field. Those who know him say that wasn't true. So did Landry. "I have strong emotional feelings," he said.

*T*om Landry looks up at the scoreboard during his final game as head coach of the Dallas Cowboys. In twenty-nine seasons as head coach, Landry led Dallas to two Super Bowl victories.

"The reason I take on the appearance of being unemotional is that I don't believe you can be emotional if you are concentrating the way you must to be effective."[4]

Jerry Jones

Despite the efforts of Schramm and Landry, the Cowboys went downhill in the 1980s. Murchison sold the team to Bum Bright in 1985, but the losing continued. Then a new face appeared on the scene. Jerry Jones stunned the sports world on February 25, 1989, by announcing that he had bought the Cowboys.

*J*erry Jones (left) and Jimmy Johnson (right) celebrate after the Cowboys win Super Bowl XXVII. Jones and Johnson were former teammates at the University of Arkansas.

He would not be a hands-off owner like Murchison, he said; he would be involved in everything, even the "socks and jocks."

Jones' most controversial move, however, was the replacement of Landry with Jimmy Johnson, Jones's old college teammate at the University of Arkansas. The change was highly unpopular with Cowboy fans. It didn't help that Dallas had a 1–15 record during Johnson's first year.

Over the years, however, Jones became one of the most powerful owners in the NFL. As a member of the Broadcasting Committee, he negotiated a huge television contract with the Fox Network. Jones is

The Dallas Cowboys Football Team

just as controversial as he is powerful. He has been criticized for signing big money deals with companies that are competitors of official NFL sponsors, and for bending the rules to sign players such as Deion Sanders to big contracts.

Jimmy Johnson

Johnson showed he was just as much a wheeler-dealer as Jones. He took complete control of the players. Those that didn't do things his way were traded or released. He was as highly emotional as Tom Landry was calm. He would become furious if the Cowboys lost. "I believe in winning," he said. "The bottom line is winning."[5]

Johnson did win. With good draft choices and shrewd trades, he built the Cowboys back into a Super Bowl champion.

Johnson was a master at firing up his team and keeping opponents off-balance, even before a game started. In 1994, during the week before the conference championship game against San Francisco, Johnson guaranteed a victory, something almost unheard of for a coach to do. His comment so angered the 49ers that they lost their composure–and the game.

Johnson's success, however, brought him into conflict with Jones. The sports world was stunned once more in March 1994, when Johnson and Jones announced that Johnson would leave the Cowboys.

*C*huck Howley was a leader of the Dallas defense, which was nicknamed Doomsday. In 1971, Howley became the only player on a losing team to win the Super Bowl MVP.

THE GLORY YEARS

F our Dallas Cowboy teams stand out above all the many great ones. Three of them won championships. The fourth great Cowboys team, maybe the best of all, never won the big one, losing championship games twice to the Green Bay Packers.

Coming Close

In 1966, Tom Landry said, "I am looking forward to this season."[1] He had good reasons. Don Meredith had matured into an outstanding quarterback. The top receiver was Bob Hayes, a former track star with blazing speed. Don Perkins and Dan Reeves were the running backs, and All-Pro tackle Ralph Neely anchored the offensive line. The defense, nicknamed Doomsday, was full of such stars as tackle Bob Lilly, linebackers Lee Roy Jordan and Chuck Howley (the only member of a losing team ever to be voted the

Super Bowl's Most Valuable Player), and defensive backs Cornell Green and Mel Renfro.

The Cowboys raced through the regular season with a 10–3–1 record. The championship game against the Packers was one of the best ever, with Green Bay winning, 34–27, after stopping a Cowboy drive at the 2-yard line in the final minute. The Cowboys were disappointed, but still confident. "We'll have our chances again," said Meredith.[2]

The very next year, the Cowboys again met Green Bay for the NFL championship. In below-zero temperatures, Dallas's hopes for their first title faded when Packer quarterback Bart Starr sneaked over for a touchdown with sixteen seconds remaining. The Packers won, 21–17, in what remains the most bitter loss in Cowboy history.

Winning the Big One

The Cowboy defense was the big story of 1971, allowing opponents only 14 points per game. In the Super Bowl, Dallas allowed Miami a record-low 185 yards total offense, whipping them, 24–3.

The offense had its moments during the Super Bowl, too. Miami was still in the game, trailing 13–3 in the third quarter, when Cowboys receiver Butch Johnson made the play of the day. He ran downfield, faked to the outside, then sped toward the end zone. Roger Staubach's 45-yard pass seemed to be too long, but Johnson leaped forward, his body fully extended, and made the grab. It was one of the most spectacular catches in Super Bowl history.

The Dallas Cowboys Football Team

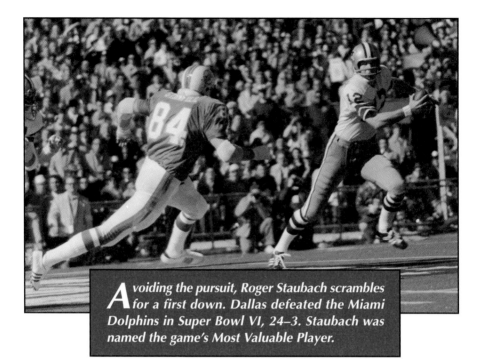

*A*voiding the pursuit, Roger Staubach scrambles for a first down. Dallas defeated the Miami Dolphins in Super Bowl VI, 24–3. Staubach was named the game's Most Valuable Player.

The victory was sweetest for Lilly. After the Super Bowl loss to Baltimore the year before, he had flung his helmet sixty yards downfield in disgust. This year was different. After the game, he lit a huge cigar and said, "Isn't it great?"[3]

Another Super Bowl

Many of the same players were around six years later when the Cowboys claimed their second Super Bowl, beating Denver, 27–10. There were new stars, however, like running back Tony Dorsett, receiver Drew Pearson, and defensive linemen Randy White, Ed "Too Tall" Jones, and Harvey Martin.

The star of the season was the defense. Opponents scored only 212 points during the Cowboys' 12–2

In 1996, the Dallas Cowboys met the Pittsburgh Steelers in Super Bowl XXX. Troy Aikman once again led the Dallas offense to victory as the Cowboys won their third Super Bowl in four years.

regular season. The three teams Dallas beat during the playoffs scored only one touchdown each. Martin was NFL Defensive Player of the Year. He and White shared the Super Bowl Most Valuable Player award.

"This team worked hard all year and paid the price," said Tom Landry. "They deserved it."[4] Renfro put it more simply: "This is the greatest Cowboy team ever."[5]

On Top Again

Dallas went through the entire decade of the 1980s without returning to the Super Bowl. Then, in the 1992 season, the new breed of Cowboys took over—Aikman, Smith, Michael Irvin, and tight end Jay Novacek performing with a huge offensive line, including Nate Newton and Erik Williams. The defense, the best in the NFL, featured Charles Haley in the line, linebacker Ken Norton, Jr., and two exciting rookies—Derrin Woodson and Kevin Smith—in the defensive backfield.

The Cowboys' overall regular-season record for the 1992 and 1993 seasons was an outstanding 25–7. Dallas capped off each year with Super Bowl victories over Buffalo, winning the two games by a combined score of 82–30. In both games, the Cowboys were able to cash in on Buffalo turnovers.

When they added a third Super Bowl victory in 1996, the Cowboys of the 1990s established themselves as one of the best teams ever. "We've done something very few teams have done," said Aikman.[6]

Dallas cornerback Larry Brown runs back the second of his two interceptions in Super Bowl XXX. For his efforts, Brown was named the game's MVP.

TEAM OF THE DECADE?

The Green Bay Packers are considered the team of the 1960s. The Pittsburgh Steelers dominated the 1970s, and the San Francisco 49ers ruled the 1980s. On January 28, 1996, the Dallas Cowboys took a giant step toward becoming the team of the 1990s by beating Pittsburgh, 27–17, in Super Bowl XXX.

It was the Cowboys' eighth appearance in the Super Bowl, more than any other team. It was their fifth Super Bowl victory, tying them with San Francisco for the all-time lead. They became the only team ever to win three Super Bowls in four years.

A Bumpy Road

The road to the championship was bumpy. Cornerback Kevin Smith was lost for the season with an injury in the first game. Defensive tackle Leon Lett and defensive back Clayton Holmes were suspended for violating the NFL's drug policy. Aikman and Coach Barry Switzer were barely speaking to one another.

Back-to-back losses in December made it look as if the Cowboys were falling apart, but they still managed a 12–4 regular-season record. They regained championship form in the playoffs, too, crushing Philadelphia and Green Bay to get to the Super Bowl.

"Every time someone counted us out, I looked to my boys on the left and to my boys on the right, and we squeezed a little tighter and pulled a little closer," said Michael Irvin. "The bottom line is that we got it done."[1]

Super Bowl XXX

Getting it done against Pittsburgh wasn't easy. With just over four minutes remaining, Pittsburgh got the ball and appeared to be driving for at least a tying field goal. Then the Steelers made a fatal mistake.

The Cowboys' defense blitzed, and wide receiver Andre Hastings, instead of adjusting his route to the outside as he was supposed to do, ran to the inside. Quarterback Neil O'Donnell threw the ball outside, right into the waiting hands of Dallas cornerback Larry Brown.

Putting It Away

Brown raced all the way down to the Steeler 6-yardline. Two plays later, Emmitt Smith blasted over to put the game out of reach.

Brown's interception, his second of the game, had saved the Cowboys. "We were hurting; we really were," said teammate Leon Lett. "We needed somebody to

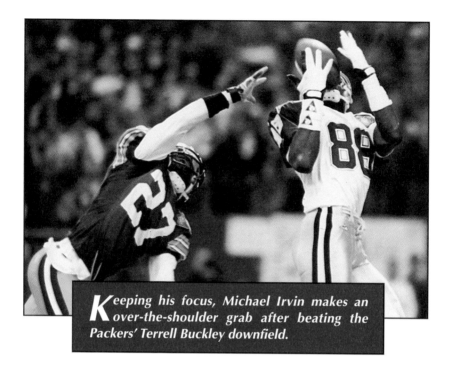

make a play, and Larry did."[2] Brown was named the game's Most Valuable Player.

Looking to the Future

Could the Cowboys continue their dominance of the NFL? It was a difficult question to answer. It is harder to keep an NFL team together than ever before. Free agency makes it easier for players to change teams. The salary cap limits the total amount of money paid to players, meaning that teams are often forced to release talented players because they earn too much.

Larry Brown, for instance, was the pride of Dallas on January 28, 1996. Less than a month later, he was an Oakland Raider. He signed a contract for $2 million,

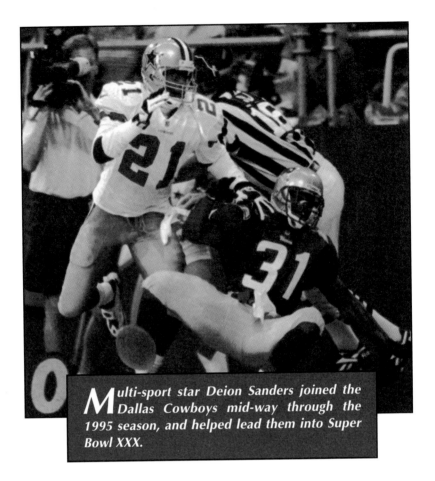

Multi-sport star Deion Sanders joined the Dallas Cowboys mid-way through the 1995 season, and helped lead them into Super Bowl XXX.

about four times what he had been paid by the Cowboys.

The Cowboys lost other players. Russell Maryland also signed with the Raiders. Linebacker Dixon Edwards went to the Minnesota Vikings. Linebacker Robert Jones signed with St. Louis. Backup offensive lineman Ron Stone became a New York Giant.

"The Packers, Steelers and 49ers kept their best players forever," said Aikman. "But the system has slowly reduced our talent base, and that will continue

The Dallas Cowboys Football Team

to happen. It's getting tougher and tougher to maintain a team that has dominance over anybody."[3]

A Good Foundation

Still, the Cowboys appear to have the tools to stay on top. The main ingredients were in place—Aikman, Irvin, and Smith are perhaps the best quarterback-receiver-running back combination ever to play on the same team. "That's why we're here, because of the talent and abilities of those players," said Switzer.[4]

The key player was Smith. His 1,773 yards rushing during the 1995 regular season led the NFL for the fourth time in five years. His 25 rushing touchdowns set a record. "They have the great back," said Pittsburgh coach Dick LeBeau, "and that's the one constant they have that separates them from the other teams."[5]

The talent didn't end there. The midseason signing of Deion Sanders had given the Cowboys perhaps the best cornerback in football. The offensive line was considered tops in the NFL.

There were questions, certainly, yet, the Cowboys seemed confident they could remain at the top. Dallas would seek to replace the players they lost through the college draft and by signing free agents of their own.

"I don't think that anyone in our organization is ready to look back over the last four years and say, 'Boy, we've really had a good run,'" said Aikman. "It's nice that this football team has made a little mark for itself, but this thing's not over yet."[6]

STATISTICS

Team Record

SEASON	SEASON RECORD	PLAYOFF RECORD	COACH	DIVISION FINISH
1960	0-11-1	—	Tom Landry	7th
1961	4-9-1	—	Tom Landry	6th
1962	5-8-1	—	Tom Landry	5th
1963	4-10	—	Tom Landry	5th
1964	5-8-1	—	Tom Landry	5th
1965	7-7	0-1	Tom Landry	2nd
1966	10-3-1	0-1	Tom Landry	1st
1967	9-5	1-1	Tom Landry	1st
1968	12-2	1-1	Tom Landry	1st
1969	11-2-1	0-1	Tom Landry	1st
1970	10-4	2-1	Tom Landry	1st
1971	11-3	3-0	Tom Landry	1st
1972	10-4	1-1	Tom Landry	2nd
1973	10-4	1-1	Tom Landry	1st
1974	8-6	—	Tom Landry	3rd
1975	10-4	2-1	Tom Landry	2nd
1976	11-3	0-1	Tom Landry	1st
1977	12-2	3-0	Tom Landry	1st
1978	12-4	2-1	Tom Landry	1st
1979	11-5	0-1	Tom Landry	1st
1980	12-4	2-1	Tom Landry	2nd
1981	12-4	1-1	Tom Landry	1st
1982	6-3	2-1	Tom Landry	2nd
1983	12-4	0-1	Tom Landry	2nd
1984	9-7	—	Tom Landry	4th
1985	10-6	0-1	Tom Landry	1st
1986	7-9	—	Tom Landry	3rd
1987	7-8	—	Tom Landry	2nd
1988	3-13	—	Tom Landry	5th
1989	1-15	—	Jimmy Johnson	5th
1990	7-9	—	Jimmy Johnson	4th
1991	11-5	1-1	Jimmy Johnson	2nd

The Dallas Cowboys Football Team

Team Record (con't)

SEASON	SEASON RECORD	PLAYOFF RECORD	COACH	DIVISION FINISH
1992	13-3	3-0	Jimmy Johnson	1st
1993	12-4	3-0	Jimmy Johnson	1st
1994	12-4	1-1	Barry Switzer	1st
1995	12-4	3-0	Barry Switzer	1st
1996	10-6	1-1	Barry Switzer	1st
1997	6-10	—	Barry Switzer	4th
1998	. 10-6	0-1	Chan Gailey	1st
1999	8-8	0-1	Chan Gailey	2nd
Totals	352-236-6	33-22		

Coaching Records

COACH	SEASONS	RECORD	CHAMPIONSHIPS
Tom Landry	1960–88	250-162-6	Capitol Division, 1967–69; NFC Eastern Division, 1973, 1976, 1979, 1981, 1985; Eastern Conference, 1966; NFC, 1970, 1975, 1978; Super Bowl VI (1971), XII (1977).
Jimmy Johnson	1989–93	44-36	Super Bowl XXVII (1992) Super Bowl XXVIII (1993)
Barry Switzer	1994–97	40-24	NFC Eastern Division, 1994, 1996. Super Bowl XXX (1995)
Chan Gailey	1998–99	33-22	NFC Eastern Division, 1998

Great Cowboys' Career Statistics

PASSING							
PLAYER	SEASONS	Y	G	ATT	COMP	YDS	TD
*Roger Staubach	1969–79	11	141	2,958	1,685	22,700	153
Danny White	1976–88	13	166	2,950	1,761	21,959	155
Troy Aikman	1989–	11	154	4,453	2,742	31,310	158
Don Meredith	1960–68	9	104	2,308	1,170	17,199	135

RUSHING							
PLAYER	SEASONS	Y	G	ATT	YDS	AVG	TD
*Tony Dorsett	1977–87	12	173	2,936	12,739	4.3	77
Emmitt Smith	1990–	10	155	3,243	13,963	4.3	136
Don Perkins	1961–68	8	107	1,500	6,217	4.1	42
Calvin Hill	1969–74	12	156	1,452	6,083	4.2	42

RECEIVING							
PLAYER	SEASONS	Y	G	REC	YDS	AVG	TD
Michael Irvin	1988–	12	159	750	11,904	15.9	65
Drew Pearson	1973–83	11	156	489	7,822	16.0	48
Tony Hill	1977–86	10	141	479	7,988	16.7	51

DEFENSE									
PLAYER	SEASONS	Y	G	TACK	AST	TOT	SACK	INT	FUM
*Randy White	1975–1988	14	209	701	403	1,104	111	1	10
*Bob Lilly	1961–1974	14	196	—	—	—	89	1	16

*Hall of Fame Members

SEASONS=Seasons with Cowboys
Y=Years in the NFL
G=Games
ATT=Attempts
YDS=Yards
COMP=Completions
AVG=Average
TD=Touchdowns
REC=Receptions
TACK=Tackles
AST=Assists
TOT=Total
SACK=Sacks
INT=Interceptions
FUM=Fumble Recoveries

CHAPTER NOTES

Chapter 1

1. Paul Zimmerman, "With Young Legs and Bold Maneuvers, the Cowboys Rolled Over the 49ers and Into the Super Bowl," *Sports Illustrated,* January 25, 1993, p. 12.

2. Mike Fisher, "Cowboys Bowl Over 49ers," *Fort Worth Star-Telegram,* January 18, 1993, p. C3.

3. "Jimmy Johnson Q&A," *Fort Worth Star-Telegram,* January 18, 1993, p. C3.

4. Fisher, p. 3.

5. Richie Whitt, "Gameday Notebook," *Fort Worth Star-Telegram,* January 18, 1993, p. C5.

6. "A Blowout by Any Other Name," *Fort Worth Star-Telegram,* January 18, 1993, p. C10.

7. Paul Zimmerman, "Big D, as in Dynasty," *Sports Illustrated,* February 8, 1993, p. 54.

Chapter 2

1. Richard Whittington, *The Dallas Cowboys* (New York: Harper & Row, 1981), p. 21.

2. Bob St. John, *Tex! The Man Who Built the Dallas Cowboys* (Englewood Cliffs, N.J.: Prentice-Hall, 1988), p. 254.

Chapter 3

1. Jeff Meyers, *Dallas Cowboys* (New York: Macmillan Publishing Co., 1974), p. 130.

2. Richard Whittington, *The Dallas Cowboys* (New York: Harper & Row, 1981), p. 191.

3. Dick Conrad, *Tony Dorsett: From Heisman to Super Bowl in One Year* (Chicago: Children's Press, 1982), p. 35.

4. Nathan Aaseng, *Football's Punishing Pass Rushers* (Minneapolis, Minn: Lerner Publications Co., 1984), p. 60.

5. Gil LeBreton, "Offense Unleashes Emmitt," *Fort Worth Star-Telegram,* October 8, 1991, p. C6.

Chapter 4

1. Bob St. John, *Tex! The Man Who Built the Dallas Cowboys* (Englewood Cliffs, N.J.: Prentice-Hall, 1988), p. 230.

2. Jeff Meyers, *Dallas Cowboys* (New York: Macmillan Publishing Co., 1974), p. 149.

3. Richard Whittington, *The Dallas Cowboys* (New York: Harper & Row, 1981), p. 203.

4. Meyers, p. 115.

5. "Jimmy Johnson, Head Coach," *Dallas Cowboys Media Guide* (Dallas, Tex.: Dallas Cowboys, 1989), p. 5.

Chapter 5

1. Richard Whittington, *The Dallas Cowboys* (New York: Harper & Row, 1981), p. 66.

2. Jeff Meyers, *Dallas Cowboys* (New York: Macmillan Publishing Co., 1974), p. 81.

3. Whittington, p. 122.

4. Ibid., p. 166.

5. Ibid.

6. Richie Whitt, "Cowboys Notebook," *Fort Worth Star-Telegram*, January 31, 1994, p. B6.

Chapter 6

1. Jean-Jacques Taylor, "Reaching Higher," *The Dallas Morning News*, February 2, 1996, p. H5.

2. Kevin Lyons, "Cornerback's Interceptions Turn Back Steelers," *Fort Worth Star-Telegram*, January 29, 1996, p. AA13.

3. Ed Werder, "Crowning Moment," *The Dallas Morning News*, January 28, 1996, p. B29.

4. Josie Karp, "To the Third Power," *Fort Worth Star-Telegram*, January 28, 1996, p. K1.

5. Dave Caldwell, "Emmit's Expectation: Carry Through the 90s," *The Dallas Morning News*, Februry 2, 1996, p. H7.

6. Jim Reeves, "Even Cowboys Have Hard Time Not Mentioning the D-Word," *Fort Worth Star-Telegram*, January 29, 1996, p. AA2.

GLOSSARY

draft—The system by which college players are chosen by NFL teams. The teams choose in turn, with the teams with the worst records getting to choose first and the better teams last.

free agency—The system that allows a player who has completed his contract with a team to be signed by any other team.

Heisman Trophy—The award given each year to the college football player considered the best in the nation.

instant replay—The system of giving an official seated in the press box the power, after viewing videotapes, to reverse decisions made by officials on the field. Instant replay is no longer used.

offensive coordinator—The assistant coach in charge of planning and executing all parts of the team's offense.

playoffs—The system of having the teams with the best records each year meet in a series of games to determine a final champion.

post—A pass pattern that calls for a receiver to cut across the middle of the football field.

Pro Bowl—A game played each year the week after the Super Bowl between teams of the best players from the National Football Conference and the American Football Conference.

salary cap—The total amount of money an owner can pay to the players on his team.

scouting—1. Watching another team play, either in person or in films, to help prepare to play that team. 2. The system of observing and evaluating college players as to their ability to play professional sports.

scrambling—This occurs when the quarterback is forced to run away from pass rushers in order to avoid being trapped for a loss.

Super Bowl—The game between the NFC and AFC champions played each year to determine the NFL championship.

FURTHER READING

Anderson, Dave. *The Story of Football.* New York: Beech Tree Books, 1985.

Gutman, Bill. *Emmitt Smith: NFL Super Runner.* Brookfield, Conn.: The Millbrook Press, 1995.

Macnow, Glen. *Sports Great Troy Aikman.* Springfield, N.J.: Enslow Publishers, Inc., 1995.

Patey, R. L. "Buddy." *The Illustrated Rules of Football.* Nashville, Tenn: Ideals Children's Books, 1995.

Savage, Jeff. *Deion Sanders: Star Athlete.* Springfield, N.J.: Enslow Publishers, Inc., 1995.

————. *Emmitt Smith: Star Running Back.* Springfield, N.J.: Enslow Publishers, Inc., 1995.

Sullivan, George. *All About Football.* New York: G. P. Putnam's Sons, 1987.

Thornley, Stew. *Deion Sanders: Prime Time Player.* Minneapolis, Minn: Lerner Publications Co., 1993.

The Dallas Cowboys Football Team

INDEX

WHERE TO WRITE

Dallas Cowboys
Cowboys Center
1 Cowboys Parkway
Irving, TX 75063-4727

WEBSITE

http://www.dallascowboys.com

The Dallas Cowboys Football Team